Autobiographies You Never
Thought You'd Read

# BIGFOOT

Catherine Chambers

raintree
a Capstone company — publishers for children

Raintree is an imprint of Capstone Global Library Limited, a company incorporated in England and Wales having its registered office at 7 Pilgrim Street, London, EC4V 6LB – Registered company number: 6695582

www.raintreepublishers.co.uk
myorders@raintreepublishers.co.uk

Edited by Linda Staniford
Designed by Steve Mead
Original illustrations © Capstone Global Library Ltd 2015
Illustrated by Ryan Petney - Advocate Art
Production by Victoria Fitzgerald
Originated by Capstone Global Library Ltd
Printed and bound in China by Leo Paper Products

ISBN 978 1 406 29626 6
19 18 17 16 15
10 9 8 7 6 5 4 3 2 1

**British Library Cataloguing in Publication Data**
A full catalogue record for this book is available from the British Library.

**Acknowledgements**
Every effort has been made to contact copyright holders of material reproduced in this book. Any omissions will be rectified in subsequent printings if notice is given to the publisher.

# Contents

Some words are shown in bold, **like this**. You can find out what they mean by looking in the glossary.

# Who am I?
# Where am I from?

I am Bigfoot. Some people call me Sasquatch. I come from North America. This map shows where people have reported seeing me in the United States and Canada.

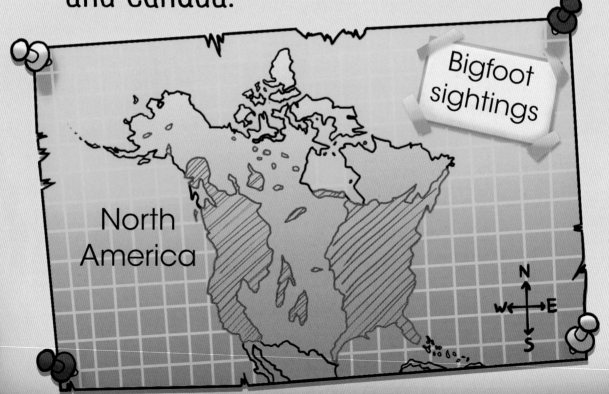

North America

Bigfoot sightings

N
W E
S

Some **American Indians** on the East Coast talk of a creature called Windigo. Others speak of Ha'yacatsi. It means "Lost Giant", because he's huge and likes to hide. But are they the same as me?

## DID YOU KNOW?

The name Sasquatch was created from American Indian names such as Sokqueatl and Soss-q'tal.

# What do I look and smell like?

Some people say I am very tall and hairy. Others say I look like a ghost or a stone giant.

But the Chickasaw people of the Southeastern woodlands talk of Lofa, a smelly, hairy beast. Now that's not very nice! Surely that's not me?

## DID YOU KNOW?

Hunters say that Bigfoot leaves a lingering bad smell wherever it goes.

# Do I live alone?

Some people think I am on my own all the time, but I have a sister. She's smaller than me and less hairy. People who have seen her say she's cleaner, too. Hmmm, I've no idea what they mean...

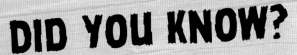

# DID YOU KNOW?

The Kwakiutl and Tlingit peoples of Northwest Canada tell tales of Tsunoqua. She's a big wild woman who lives in the woods.

# How old am I?

It's hard to tell my age. But as I get older I start to stoop. My hair turns grey and dangles off my body. Well, that's what humans say. **American Indians** have been telling tales about me and my family for years.

## DID YOU KNOW?

Hunters say they have seen Bigfoot with black or red-brown hair.

# How do I move?

My legs are long but never straight. I move smoothly on my two legs, using long strides. Some say I can run as fast as a horse!

# DID YOU KNOW?

An adult Bigfoot footprint is said to be about 38 centimetres (15 inches) long. Its stride can reach 1.5 metres (5 feet).

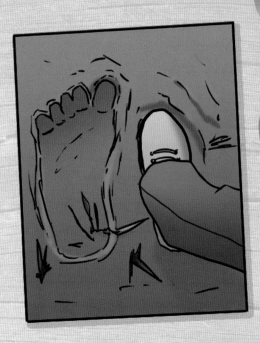

# Where do I live?

I live mostly in thick woodland. Humans say they have found my food waste in caves, too. But I'm keeping the location of my home a secret.

I like to wander near rivers and lakes.
You might even see me enjoying a swim.

# What do I eat?

My parents taught me how to find nuts and berries. Some humans say I kill deer or even pet dogs and cats.

The Comanche people of the Southern Plains tell tales of Mu Pitz, a **cannibal** monster. Is that really me? I don't think so.

## DID YOU KNOW?

Some hunters say they have found stashes of corn stolen by Bigfoot.

# Do I hibernate?

Some humans think I store food for winter **hibernation**. It's certainly hard to hunt and gather in dark, chilly months. So I store fat in a hump on my back to help me through.

But I don't hibernate. You might find my footprints in the snow! I hide and watch hunters tracking them!

# Am I fierce?

I think I'm a really nice guy. But some people say we like to throw rocks. And some even claim that Tsunoqua, the wild woman, roasts children and eats them! Terrible tales like this might scare you away from folks like us!

# DID YOU KNOW?

Some people say that European **tree fellers** heard old tales like Tsunoqua's around the camp fire. Did these people make up Bigfoot based on what they'd heard?

# Am I a ghost?

The Kwakiutl people of Vancouver Island, Canada, believe in a big ghostly creature. They call him Bukwus, which means the wild Ghost Chief from the woods. According to these people, Bukwus likes to offer humans some of his food. Then he turns them into a Bukwus too! Could Bukwus be me?

## DID YOU KNOW?

Kwakiutl artists carve colourful Bukwus masks. They are worn during ceremonies and **solemn** dances.

# Are these tales real?

Are these real tales or tall tales? My grandma says that 100 years ago there was a teacher called J.W. Burns. He collected stories about wild men, who he named Sasquatch.

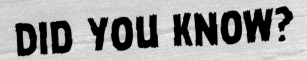

# DID YOU KNOW?

Many clubs today organize Bigfoot hunts. They use cameras and electrical equipment to look for him.

# Have you spotted me?

You think you've spotted me, but have you really? Some of you say you've found my footprints. My knuckle prints, too. Even my poo! Is it true? Or am I just smarter than you?

# DID YOU KNOW?

There have been many fake Bigfoot finds, from bears' fur to footprints made with plaster models!

# Do I really exist?

Of course, I believe I exist. I even have family in other parts of the world. My **Yeti** cousins live in the **Himalayan** mountain range. Others live in Africa.

You can tell we are related. We are all big, hairy and very shy. I hope humans will never harm us.

## DID YOU KNOW?

Some say that Bigfoot is descended from an ancient great ape called Gigantopithecus.

# Glossary

**American Indian** first people who arrived in America thousands of years ago

**cannibal** creature that eats other creatures of its own kind

**hibernation** when the body slows down a lot in winter. Some creatures sleep through the winter.

**Himalaya** mountain range in Asia

**tree feller** someone who cuts down trees

**solemn** very serious

**Yeti** huge hairy creature like a Bigfoot but found in Himalayan mountains

# Find out more

You could find out more about Bigfoot and Bigfoot hunters in other books and on the internet.

## Books

*Bigfoot and Other Mysteries,* John Townsend (Ticktock, 2008)
You will find out more about Bigfoot and other mysteries in this book.

*Looking For Bigfoot* (Step into Reading Level 4), Bonnie Worth (Random House, 2010)
This book tells the tale of a Bigfoot sighting.

*The Unsolved Mystery of Bigfoot* (First Facts), Michael Burgan (Capstone Press, 2013)
Find out more facts about the Bigfoot legend in this book.

## Websites

Learn more about ancient humans and great apes on these websites:

www.nhm.ac.uk/nature-online/life/human-origins/early-human-family/index.html

www.bbc.co.uk/nature/life/Hominidae

# Index